"Is it just me?"

A Canadian Conservative's unapologetic thoughts about 21st Century North American Life

Copyright © 2021 by Grant Moore
All rights reserved.

Possible Back or Inside Cover Quotes:

"Pro-choice enthusiasts think that abortion is okay but that suicidal people should be given help because, you know, a life is a terrible thing to waste."

"Canada's quest for unity is not helped by a national media that seems to have as its task the continual stirring of the pot to keep immigrants and visible minorities in a state of anger by constantly reprising everything bad that has ever happened."

"Media bias and Big Tech censorship and de-platforming is truly outrageous, given that the American taxpayer supports these elite corporations with, among other things, an urban infrastructure, a military, patent law, contract law, an educational system, and a consumer base."

"Way to go America: you got rid of your greatest president in exchange for your worst. Say what you want about Donald Trump but at least he was popular with some portion of the American electorate, 75 million-plus actually.

Joe Biden is not popular with anyone. He has no capacity to lead the country, to occupy the bully pulpit, to rally those he serves in difficult times, and to provide moral and spiritual leadership.

It's kind of a problem, you know. Anyone who has spent time in the school system knows that the best teachers can command the attention of the students. If a teacher can't do this, nothing else really matters. Donald Trump can command America's attention. Joe Biden can't."

"Forget life in the hood: young Black males are more likely to die installing solar panels than via interactions with the police."

"The liberal left has a deep and abiding faith in anti-racist education. Racism, they believe, is always rooted in irrational prejudices or is the poisonous legacy of a troubled upbringing. It is unrelated to the reality of everyday life and never the product of rational thought. They're wrong."

"There is so much talk about handgun bans and gun control but perhaps some review should be given to rap music as a form of hate speech. It certainly seems to incite levels of violence comparable to drug dealing, if the murders and mayhem of recent decades in North America are any indication."

"No empirical study exists showing the benefits of diversity, it is all just rationalization (hamster treadmill spinning). In fact, the entire modern world was largely created by a non-diverse group of dead white males living approximately from London to Berlin."

"I would like to see more diversity. Let's have more heterosexuals employed in the interior design and fashion industries. And how about Big Tech break down barriers by hiring older people (i.e., over the age of 40) with conservative political views?"

"The idea that homogeneous groups are less creative and less insightful than diverse ones is ridiculous. Also ridiculous is that they are more prone to group think and less likely to question faulty assumptions. In fact, racially diverse college and university campuses in North America are the epitome of group think and the epitome of lack of individuality."

"The GLBTQ community comprises less than 5 percent of the North American population with gays and lesbians being perhaps 1-2 percent each. That's it. But turn on Netflix and search for lesbian content and the line-up is longer than the queue at a Texas foodbank."

"The modern-day Olympics have expanded and mutated to be unrecognizable from their roots and not just because of rampant commercialism and the participation of professionals. Almost anything now qualifies as an "Olympic" event: games (golf); outdoor vacation activities (kayaking, beach volleyball); hobbies (climbing, surfing, sailing.)"

"Today's music is not that great anyway, to put it mildly. The music video with the obligatory aerobics-workout back-up dancers has been done to death. Otherwise, it's boring and overdone, the artists themselves pretentious, scripted, choreographed, lip-synced, auto-tuned and contrived, who change their public image every other week. They are not real musicians; they are just marketing schemes. Their four-tone "music" is barfed out mostly by some computer programmer in Sweden apparently."

"Everybody marries the wrong person: there is no "right" person for anyone despite what the YouTube videos and relationship counsellors would have you believe. If you cannot accept this, you cannot be married."

"I am optimistic for the future and future generations because deep down I think we know that what Western society has done in recent decades is not empowering. Abandoning the guidance of our past and embracing hedonism and subjectivity was not some genius idea. "

"Women in the entertainment industry (when they're not in rehab) can serially date, hook-up, have affairs, have multiple breakups and multiple marriages, perform on stage in leather bathing suits or lingerie, and broaden their sexual identities to include both men and women.

But don't dare assume they are easy and approach them with cheap come-ons. They resent men who do that ---- unless of course the men are rich, famous, good-looking or can help their career. Then it's okay."

"Celebrities like to go on talk shows and discuss their "issues". They are welcome on all shows as long as they are willing to attack Donald Trump. Most are able to summon the courage to do so."

"YouTube used to feature a charming, rustic collection of guitar lessons, collectors and hobbyists, home handymen, magicians, lecturers, moms in the kitchen etc. Now it's basically a toxic, soft-porn site overrun by Kardashian/Jenner-wannabees who are willing to say anything, do anything or confess anything (e.g., "how many people have you slept with --- relatives don't count") for their fifteen minutes of fame."

"History will likely trace America's peak as having occurred in the first few decades after the Second World War, a time of egalitarianism when life offered abundant opportunities".

"Harvard practices bad meritocracy that is corrupted by nepotism and diversity admits, but New York City's schools practice true meritocracy in admission to the most sought-after schools. It doesn't get any fairer than going strictly by standardized test results."

"One of the great things about America is that it always finds ways to make the rich even richer and extend more privileges to the already-privileged. And its not just favorable tax treatment and celebrity endorsement deals"

INTRODUCTION

This book is a collection of my thoughts, observations, jottings, unpublished scholarly articles, and unpublished letters to the editor from recent years. Most have been fleshed out and updated to some degree.

Canada and the United States are the focus of this book, but some issues have wider relevance.

I am a conservative but not an idealogue. My core moral values and duties are rooted in my Christian faith and I try to develop my position on political and social issues through logic and common sense.

I am perfectly willing to change my mind if compelling argumentation arises. I am not wedded irredeemably to uncompromising and dogmatic positions, certainly not in the realm of social and political issues.

Someone once said that "when everyone is thinking the same no one is thinking". It amazes me, but also troubles me, at the convergence of thought that has occurred at North American colleges and universities where liberalism and the Progressive Left have taken over and conservative voices are unwelcome and even ridiculed and persecuted. How can that possibly be a good thing? How can young students --- tomorrow's leaders --- develop sober second thoughts and a healthy scepticism of received wisdom if opposing voices are stifled and even de-platformed?

I hope that the writings in this book will cause readers to thoughtfully re-examine their own views on social and political life in North America and have a few laughs along the way.

My efforts at humour are purely intentional.

Grant Moore
Mississauga, Ontario
March 2021

TABLE OF CONTENTS

CHAPTER 1: SEX AND GENDER — PAGE

SECTION 1.1	Women in Non-Traditional Occupations	1
SECTION 1.2	Gay Pride Parades	2
SECTION 1.3	Gays and Lesbians having Kids.	3
SECTION 1.4	Abortion	3
SECTION 1.5	I'm coming out as a hyper-heterosexual.	4
SECTION 1.6	Why BBW but not BBM?.	5

CHAPTER 2: POLITICAL LIFE AND PUBLIC POLICY — PAGE

SECTION 2.1	Rich Versus Poor	6
SECTION 2.2	Canada and Gun Control	7
SECTION 2.3	Right to bear arms in Canada	7
SECTION 2.4	Vehicle Window Tints.	9
SECTION 2.5	Canada's Quest for Unity.	9
SECTION 2.6	Immigration.	10
SECTION 2.7	The Mainstream Media (MSM)	12
SECTION 2.8	The Progressive Left and the Trump era	13
SECTION 2.9	Joe Biden: The President Nobody Wants.	15
SECTION 2.10	COVID-19 and the extended family.	18
SECTION 2.11	The Christmas Tree.	20

CHAPTER 3: RACE AND MINORITIES   PAGE

SECTION 3.1	Black Lives Matter: Why are people protesting?	.21
SECTION 3.2	The Advancement of Minorities	.22
SECTION 3.3	Racism	.23
SECTION 3.4	Anti-Black racism	.24
SECTION 3.5	Who will want to teach in Peel?	.25
SECTION 3.6	Public comments on police 'street check' law	.26
SECTION 3.7	To Kill a Mockingbird	.27
SECTION 3.8	Slavery in America	.28
SECTION 3.9	Samuel Opuku	.29
SECTION 3.10	Is Rap Music a Form of Hate Speech?	.29
SECTION 3.11	Diversity: Part 1	.30
SECTION 3.12	Diversity: Part 2	.32
SECTION 3.13	Be a Better Friend to Career Felons	.35

CHAPTER 4: SPORTS   PAGE

SECTION 4.1	The Olympic Games: Cancel them for good.	.37
SECTION 4.2.1	The National Football League: Part 1	.38
SECTION 4.2.2	The National Football League: Part 2	.40
SECTION 4.2.3	The National Football League: Part 3	.42
SECTION 4.2.4	The National Football League: Part 4	.43
SECTION 4.3	Membership Meeting – Augusta National Golf Club.	.47

CHAPTER 5: RELATIONSHIPS — PAGE

SECTION 5.1	Do not Marry the Wrong Person.	.48
SECTION 5.2	What does it mean do be "in a relationship"?	50
SECTION 5.3	Open Relationships	.50
SECTION 5.4	Stop trying to make women like you..	.51
SECTION 5.5	Young Men and Marriage	.52

CHAPTER 6: ENTERTAINMENT — PAGE

SECTION 6.1	Sex and the City – The TV Show	.55
SECTION 6.2	How to be a Female Stand-up Comic	.56
SECTION 6.3	Hollywood and the #MeToo Movement.	.57
SECTION 6.4	Late-Night Talk Shows	.59
SECTION 6.5	Celebrities "Sharing"	.60
SECTION 6.6	YouTubers	.61
SECTION 6.7	School Admission by Merit	.65
SECTION 6.8	Privileges for the Already-Privileged	.66
SECTION 6.9	Positive Role Models for Kids	.67

CHAPTER 7: CANADIAN IMMIGRATION POLICY — PAGE

SECTION 7.1	The Century Initiative and 100 Million Canadians by the Year 2100.	.69

Chapter 1

SEX AND GENDER

1.1 Women in Non-Traditional Occupations

Yes, let us encourage girls to aspire to be firefighters where their diminutive size and lack of upper-body strength gives them a natural competitive advantage over male candidates.

It is interesting that concern with the advancement of women is selective to the point of being almost surgical in application. It is important for women to be doctors, lawyers, school principals, police officers and now firefighters, but beyond that there are dozens, nay hundreds, of professions and occupations where women are virtually non-existent, and nobody gives a hoot. The list would include hydro-transmission linemen, plumbers, carpenters, electricians, HVAC technicians, bricklayers, iron workers, heavy equipment operators, miners, salvage divers, and on and on and on.

No one hectors the longshoreman's unions, the Merchant Marine, or the Coast Guard, demanding to know why women are underrepresented on the docks or on vessels plying the world's oceans and inland waterways. There are no angry picketers outside automobile dealerships protesting the virtual nonexistence of female mechanics. And no outreach programs exist in our high schools to encourage girls to become welders, stonemasons, or long-haul truck drivers.

We are told that women can do anything men can do. So, why don't they?

1.2 Gay Pride Parades

I wonder whether Gay Pride parades are an idea whose time has gone. At this point, are we really making new converts, breaking down barriers, and increasing public sensitivity? All I read about in Toronto and other cities is deficits and in-fighting.

If you are a "queer, gender-nonconforming person," then you should probably get used to the fact that — regarding this aspect of your personality — you are different from most people. Probably the rest of the world is not all that fascinated with the fabulousness of who and what you are.

But Hollywood just won't let up. It pushes homosexuality as if it's something that normal people find interesting and actually want to waste a single cycle thinking about. It's just indoctrination by repetition. Condition people against their normal revulsion. And no one ever explains why the capacity to be attracted to and love the same-sex or even both sexes are more noteworthy than being born left-handed. Why is being gay spun as some sort of talent or achievement?

Sorry, homosexuality is nothing to "celebrate". It's just a biological malfunction. All this propaganda is like "Cancer: The Musical". Hey, some cells are just different!

And the idea of LGBTQ movement solidarity is laughable. Gay men generally find lesbians boring, frumpy, and humorless, and lesbians consider gay men, particularly flamboyant gay men, as a sort of ditzy second cousins, to be laughed at but not taken seriously.

Gays and lesbians really are not interested in each other at all. Why would they be?

1.3 Gays and Lesbians having Kids.

Liberals never make any sense.

Gay marriage enthusiasts say that homosexuality is just as legitimate as real sexuality. But homosexuality cannot produce children, and so gays must rely on heterosexuals to have kids of 'their own'. Though the kids were created by heterosexuality, homosexuals and liberals pretend as though the 'gays had the kids'.

Same with affirmative action. Liberals say it's 'racist' to say some races are smarter than others. Yet, it promotes affirmative action which is premised on the conviction that some races are indeed less capable than others. Huh?

1.4 Abortion

Pro-choice enthusiasts think that abortion is okay but that suicidal people should be given help because, you know, a life is a terrible thing to waste.

Further complicating matters is *The Unborn Victims of Violence Act of 2004* (Public Law 108-212), a United States law which recognizes an embryo or fetus in utero as a legal victim, if they are injured or killed during the commission of any of over 60 listed federal crimes of violence. The law defines "child in utero" as "a member of the species Homo sapiens, at any stage of development, who is carried in the womb."

In certain circumstances then, a baby is transformed into a human being, their death of which can be prosecuted. On November 12, 2004, California resident Scott Peterson was convicted of first-degree murder for his wife Laci's death and second-degree murder for the death of his unborn son Conner.

A woman has the right to control over her body and it is no one else's business, including the child's father. Unless of course she decides to keep the baby in which case he can pay child support for years.

And can somebody explain how a media that champions transexuals and abortion can believe that people should be talked out of killing themselves but not chopping off their penis or murdering a baby?

1.5 I'm coming out as a hyper-heterosexual.

I always knew that I was hetero, from the earliest days of puberty when I started to like girls in a way that was different than before.

I liked girls for one reason: they weren't boys. Girls on their journey to womanhood were wonderful creatures: they had long silky hair, they smelled great, their skin was way soft, they had curves, and reproductive capabilities designed for me. They were amazing. I still think so.

Boys? I had some great male friends but feeling a physical attraction for them was beyond the pale. Why the hell would I like them in that way: they had everything I already had: chest muscles, body hair, and external genitalia. I never thought that a penis was all that attractive (particularly uncircumcised) and I sure as hell didn't want another one for any reason.

I don't even like being around naked men in the change rooms at health clubs and I'm not homophobic at all. Still, I was social-distancing from naked men long before it became fashionable via COVID-19. Better not to take a chance of developing homo-erotic thoughts.

So, I came out as a hyper-heterosexual: I'm 150 percent straight and minus 50 percent gay. Thankfully, my parents were supportive.

I remember my dad said "Grant, if you like girls your mother and I will stand behind you. You're still our son."

I'm looking forward to the talk-show circuit where I can "open-up" about "my issues" But don't be a hater or I'll have to "call you out" and "clap back" at you.

1.6 Why BBW but not BBM?

A Big Beautiful Woman (BBW) is a euphemism for an overweight woman.

The term BBW has been around for years, apparently coined by Carole Shaw in 1979 when she launched *BBW Magazine*. It is now well-established in the vernacular and can be found in common usage in personal ads and online dating services.

There is no shortage of synonyms to describe BBWs: chesty, busty, husky, big-boned, Rubenesque and full-figured, among others. Men, on the other hand, are just fat.

Many large women have achieved success as models and their message has been that weight is nothing to be ashamed of and that large women can do just fine if they dress and groom appropriately and carry themselves well.

So why are there no Big Beautiful Men in the fashion industry? I cannot recall ever seeing an overweight man in any type of ad. Overweight men are just obese --- fat slobs who eat too much junk food and watch too much TV. No one thinks that men with beer bellies should do anything except put the fork down.

I see discrimination here.

Chapter 2

POLITICAL LIFE AND PUBLIC POLICY

2.1 Rich Versus Poor

If present trends continue the lucky few with inherited wealth and political connections can pretend that they earned their privileged positions. But even they are afraid somebody is going to harm or kill them and steal their precious stuff, so they segregate themselves from the rest of society and live in a parallel universe, forgetting that most people do not live like they do.

In the United States, these rifts and mutual animosities that are constantly being reinforced by the mainstream media and the Progressive left will not just evaporate one day – none of the tribes will surrender and agree to be the other's slave.

A society with no shared values that eschews compromise, and a sense of collective responsibility is not sustainable. It is a failed state waiting to happen and that is where America is heading.

Maybe it is Gaddafi's revenge from the afterlife because it sure looks like future of the United States is going to resemble an Americanized version of post-2012 Libya.

2.2 Canada and Gun Control

Canada has reached the limit of what can be achieved with gun control. It is already an ordeal for law-abiding citizens to acquire firearms and yet the federal Liberals have promised to ban AR-15s and all other "military-style assault rifles" even though, according to the Canadian Coalition for Firearms Rights, no licensed gun owner has ever committed a crime using an AR-15 in Canada.[1]

Reform needs to occur in the criminal justice system. One thing we could use is some hanging judges. Even the Supreme Court of Canada seems to agree. In a decision released in the fall of 2019 the Court held that Canadian judges have been too soft on punishment for 30 years in giving offenders the lowest possible sentence that applied at any time between their crime and their sentencing. And using the punishment most favourable to the accused had occurred in many contexts, even regarding convicted murderers' wait for parole eligibility.[2]

Another reform to consider is so-called "three strikes" legislation as exists in some American states where repeat offenders with multiple felonies (i.e., serious crimes punishable by imprisonment more than one year) can be incarcerated for life. Criminologists know that violent crimes such as assault, break-and-enter, and robbery are often the preparatory stage for homicides. Why doesn't Canada's criminal justice system seem to know this? If it did, it is reasonable to conclude that there would be fewer murders committed by young men out on the streets with long criminal histories.

2.3 Right to bear arms in Canada

It is well known that the Second Amendment to the United States Constitution includes the right of individuals to bear arms for self-defense. It has been said that the Second Amendment wisely backs up the First Amendment, i.e., freedom of speech.

But what about Canada?

The right to bear arms has existed in English common law for at least 300 years and is imported into Canadian law by the preamble of the British North America Act, 1867 and section 26 of The Canadian Charter of Rights and Freedoms. The purpose of section 26 is to ensure that any rights or freedoms not expressly spelled out in the Charter, but which exist otherwise (including traditional rights) are not extinguished because of that omission.

The first explicit recognition of the right to bear arms in British-Canadian law occurs in the 1689 Bill of Rights. It is re-affirmed by the celebrated Blackstone in his Commentaries as one of the five most important rights of British subjects; and confirmed in several 18th and 19th century precedents.

Although this right is subject to regulation by parliament, in 1990 the Supreme Court of Canada affirmed that regulation of a right does not automatically extinguish the right. The right to bear arms is thus an historical right of all Canadians; affirmed by section 26 of the Charter: the phrase "keep arms" was for centuries in England commonly understood to denote ownership of arms by private citizens for private purposes.

Also, Canadians rights to self-defense and to bear arms are enshrined in Section 7 of the Charter, which states "Everyone has the right to life, liberty and security of the person, and the right not to be deprived thereof except in accordance with the principles of fundamental justice."

In conclusion, Canadians still retain a right to keep and bear arms -- a right grouped with all the other rights Canada adopted from England that have passed through to Canadians over the years. That right is extinguishable due to the supremacy of Parliament in the Canadian system of governance, but to this date no parliament has ever acted to pass legislation extinguishing that right.

2.4 Vehicle Window Tints

Police Services in Greater Toronto regularly launch crackdowns and blitzes to target impaired driving, speeding, or distracted driving. How about some attention paid as well to the proliferation of vehicles with illegal levels of window tints?

I regularly see vehicles with tints on all windows which completely obscure the driver and other occupants. This is not only anti-social and creepy but dangerous. Who's driving the vehicle: a Bassett hound or a twelve-year old boy whose parents are away?

I suppose part of the attraction of window tinting is privacy except that if you're out in public you're not entitled to privacy.

Cell phones, headphones, earbuds, and car window tints: modern man's tools in the pursuit of loneliness and isolation

2.5 Canada's Quest for Unity

Canada's quest for unity is not helped by a national media that seems to have as its task the continual stirring of the pot to keep immigrants and visible minorities in a state of anger by constantly reprising everything bad that has ever happened.

The media eagerly report racist tirades in stores, parking lots, fast-food restaurants, or insensitive remarks made in small towns in the Maritimes and conflate these isolated incidents as evidence of the country's unmastered racist past. Naturally, the answer is for more introspection, sensitivity training and anti-racist hectoring.

The problem is that diversity is not interesting anymore -- we are 10-20 years past that point. There is so much of it now in our largest cities that no one even knows what constitutes a minority: in many Greater Toronto neighbourhoods and schools' non-whites outnumber others by a wide margin. And, unfortunately, there's too much violent crime for any romantic notions of multiculturalism to be re-kindled.

Canadians are no more racist than in the past, probably less so, but they are cranky and when the water hole shrinks the animals look at each other differently. And the water hole has shrunk, as the non-availability of affordable housing and rental accommodation reaches near-crisis levels.

2.6 Immigration

Canadians want a re-think of the country's immigration policies.

An Angus Reid Institute survey conducted in July 2019 showed a spike in opposition to immigration, with 49 per cent of respondents calling for levels to be decreased. Only 6 per cent believed that immigration should be increased.

The survey was followed almost immediately by former-Tory MP (now "People's Party of Canada" leader) Maxime Bernier's contention that identity politics promotes an endless splintering of the population into ever-narrower shards of interest groups. And in the Quebec General Election held October 1, 2018 the Coalition Avenir Quebec (CAQ) attained power on a platform that included reduction in immigrant numbers along with a values and language test for newcomers.

At least in part, Canadian attitudes mirror the strains in the Western world in recent years around immigration and related issues of multiculturalism, religious tolerance, and refugee settlement. Unease with the status quo resulted in a resurgent nationalism in many European countries, sentiment which quickly spread to Canada and the United States.

But domestic issues are in-play as well. Canada's major immigrant-receiving municipalities now suffer soaring house prices, soaring rents, and dismal commute times. And two issues that no one ever mentions are, first, the effect that immigration/multiculturalism has had on Canada's historically-disadvantaged communities and, second, the impact on the status of the French Language outside of Quebec.

Large and robust Chinese and East-Indian populations now outnumber Canada's First Nation and Black populations who are pushed further back in line in the competition for a place in our national consciousness.

Meanwhile, as the threat of separatism has receded, and as multiculturalism has simultaneously been embraced, bilingualism has stagnated for francophones in Quebec and is on the decline for anglophones outside the province. Compared to twenty-five years ago, how many Canadians today would single-out French/English bilingualism as a central feature of Canada's identity?

So, there are legitimate issues with our immigration program, issues which deserve a civil reply and serious discussion. Unfortunately, our federal government has done an abysmal job of articulating a vision for immigration besides "more of the same" and, even then, scant effort to build public support has been forthcoming. Little wonder the Angus Reid poll numbers are as dismal as they are.

With any luck, Canadians can look forward to reasoned and stimulating debate on future immigration policy in the next federal election cycle. We deserve it.

2.7 The Mainstream Media (MSM)

There are basically five (5) ways the MSM slants the news:

1) Omission, e.g., just not reporting black-on-white crime, or not blowing it up to the degree it does alleged "racist" incidents.

2) Use of colorful adjectives, e.g., conservative politicians are "far right" with "controversial" and "extreme" ideas who appeal to "less educated" voters with "hot button issues," and

3) The "raising questions" gambit, where there's really no proof of anything going on "but this triple hearsay does 'raise questions'" sufficient to generate a sensational headline. (The best example of this is the left's obsession with "Russia" somehow causing the defeat of Hillary Clinton in 2016)

4) Interviewing only those people they know will agree with them.

5) Disabling the "comment" feature of on-line articles so that readers who might object are neutralized. This is the journalistic equivalent of the drive-by shooting.

Of course, these days the main way to manage the news is to simply ignore items that you don't like and focus on those that fit your political bias. (See CNN, MSNBC, The Washington Post and The New York Times). Use Big Tech to censor or de-platform those who insist on free speech and full and informed debate i.e., conservatives.

(Media bias and Big Tech censorship and de-platforming is truly outrageous, given that the American taxpayer supports these elite corporations with, among other things, an urban infrastructure, a military, patent law, contract law, an educational system, and a consumer base.)

The media can always claim that they can't report everything: they have limited space in their newspapers and magazines, and limited numbers of journalists on staff to develop stories. And, in any event, the relative importance of news items is subjective and requires an editor's judgement.

However, if they must report something, creative headline spin always works.

Example:

Obama as president: *"President Obama Demonstrates Bold, Decisive Leadership as He Destroys World's Leading Terrorist."*

Trump as president: *"Trump Kills Senior Iranian Official in Reckless Military Misadventure in the Middle East."*

Another technique is to link someone you dislike with embarrassing news, to wit:

Obama as president: *"Defense Department under fire for horrific cost-overruns on new weapon systems deployment."*

Trump as president: *"Trump Administration under fire for horrific cost-overruns on new weapon systems deployment.*

2.8 The Progressive Left and the Trump era

Islamism and Progressive liberalism both have submission as core tenets of their ideology. But the Progressive Left of the Democratic party cares less about the implications of Islam when practiced enthusiastically than the opportunity it presents to cast Americans as racist, xenophobic, etc.

It's practically the Democratic past time to condemn fellow citizens who don't share their views and propose various ways to punish them for their heresy.

They (and they alone) are possessed of the truth. Since the truth is known, listening to other voices is a waste of time and can be seen as counter-productive and even divisive. Conservatives can thus be portrayed as "Enemies of the People" (Hmm.. where have we heard that before)? Hence, "Cancel Culture".

One consequence of cancel culture no one mentions is that, whether via avoidance or de-platforming, civic life becomes boring. A reluctance to engage in moral, spiritual, and political argument (and an often-non-judgmental stance toward values) has exacted a heavy price: it has drained America's public discourse of moral and civic energy, and contributed to the technocratic, managerial politics afflicting many Western nations today.

The conduct of federal politics in the Trump era deteriorated so badly that objective truth became an early casualty. The great issues of the day were little discussed or even considered relevant. Congressional Democrats became motivated solely by winning rather than being guided by a moral compass and ephemeral notions of right and wrong. They refused to compromise nor acknowledge any sense of collective responsibility.

And so, in an all-out effort to destroy the Trump presidency, Democrats pursued a war-without-mercy strategy which could have been scripted from the viciousness of the Pacific war against the Japanese. No quarter asked, and none given. (Read John Dowser's terrific book *War Without Mercy.*)

Thus, after the Russian and Ukrainian collusion scandals came up empty, President Trump was impeached for the first time on December 18, 2019. The two articles of impeachment were abuse of power and obstruction of Congress neither of which is actually a crime. Trump was acquitted on February 5, 2020 when the Senate blew the whistle on this silly farce.

But no comic opera would be complete without a final act. The second impeachment charged that Trump "incited an insurrection" even though the only thing he actually said was to go to the Capitol and "peacefully and patriotically make sure that your voices are heard."

And so, in the words of Conrad Black, the House Democrats "launched an impeachment of the president with no argument, no evidence, no witnesses, no due process of any kind, for a proposed trial to remove the president from office well after he will have departed that office at the expiry of his constitutionally fixed term and to do so for conduct that did not occur."[1]

It wasn't even much of an insurrection, more like a panty raid from a college frat house. With re-telling by the mainstream media, of course, it became the Normandy invasion or the first day of the Battle of the Somme. But the fact of the matter is that the Capital Hill protestors were unarmed, threatened no one, attempted no coup, and issued no manifesto.

Compare this to the events of the summer of 2020 where the liberal media ignored months of "peaceful protests" across the country that killed scores of people, injured 700 police, and did $2 billion of damage to mainly minority-owned businesses. However, the riots, arson and looting occurred mainly in Democrat states and cities, so it was okay.

What will Trump be accused of next: square dance calling?

2.9 Joe Biden: The President Nobody Wants

Way to go America: you got rid of your greatest president in exchange for your worst. Say what you want about Donald Trump but at least he was popular with **some** portion of the American electorate, 75 million-plus actually.

---

[1] Black, Conrad. Trump's incomparable presidency. National Post 16 January 2021.

Joe Biden is not popular with anyone. He has no capacity to lead the country, to occupy the bully pulpit, to rally those he serves in difficult times, and to provide moral and spiritual leadership.

It's kind of a problem, you know. Anyone who has spent time in the school system knows that the best teachers can command the attention of the students. If a teacher can't do this, nothing else really matters. Donald Trump can command America's attention. Joe Biden can't.

The November 3rd, 2020 American Presidential election was a contest between the incumbent president, Donald Trump, and the Democratic challenger, *Not Trump* (i.e., Joe Biden).

We were told that Biden won the election, and that voter fraud did not occur. But that's really hard to believe for twelve (12) reasons:

1. Trump won the presidential debates by consensus opinion.
2. Trump was ahead in the polls on election day.
3. Trump had the approval of almost 92 percent of Republican primary delegates.
4. Trump was the incumbent president and incumbents are returned to office about ninety percent of the time.
5. Biden was so unpopular even within the Democratic party that he almost lost the primary: his final delegate total was just 68 percent.
6. Biden's running mate, Kamala Harris, was so unpopular that she dropped out of the race for the Democrat presidential nomination on December 3rd, 2019, long before the first primary in Iowa held February 3rd, 2020.
7. Trump was campaigning regularly while Biden was sequestered in his basement for long periods.
8. Wherever Trump spoke he was greeted by thousands of enthusiastic supporters.

9. Wherever Biden spoke he was greeted by, at best, handfuls of supporters and occasionally none at all - - - most of his rallies could be held in a phone booth and still allow for social distancing.

10. There often were more Trump supporters than Biden supporters at Biden rallies.

11. All of the allegations of voter fraud occurred in the key counties in six key battleground states: Nevada, Georgia, Arizona, Michigan, Wisconsin, Pennsylvania.

12. Trump won Florida, Ohio, and Iowa and only once before has a presidential candidate won these three states yet failed to win the general election: (that one time was Richard Nixon in 1960.)

It gets worse. Big tech almost immediately censored and de-platformed any mention of electoral fraud. The leftish mainstream media cooperated enthusiastically and flushed the scandal down the memory hole, aided and abetted by the late-night talk show circuit. Electoral fraud was gleefully replaced by the Capitol Hill panty raid/riot.

This issue is much too complicated for the average person to discern the truth. Allegations involve fraudulent ballots, ballot harvesting, computer glitches, improper voter identifications, violations of state law, feckless legislatures and state supreme courts, and so on.

What is really needed is a forensic audit conducted by a bi-partisan committee or by a Special Counsel. Since there are no investigative journalists a la Woodward and Bernstein who want to look into the matter, something more must be done.

A twenty-first century equivalent of the Warren Commission and its progeny *Report of The President's Commission on the Assassination of President Kennedy* would be perfect. This much-maligned document did, in fact, get it right, proving beyond all doubt that Lee Harvey Oswald was the assassin and that he acted alone.

2.10 COVID-19 and the extended family

Members of the baby-boom generation will recall growing up that the nuclear family seemed to be the Canadian norm. Maternal and paternal grandparents each had their own homes as often did older siblings who moved out the family home and into an apartment at the earliest opportunity. Many venues were thus available for family get-togethers to celebrate holidays, birthdays, and other social occasions.

But as it turned out, the nuclear family was an anomaly of a few decades in the post-World War II period. For most of Canada's history the extended family was more the norm, with an older, retired parent (or parents) living with a son or daughter and his/her spouse and children.

Living with extended family, which includes parents and other relatives outside the immediate family, is more common in Asia, the Middle East, South America, and Sub-Saharan African cultures.

It certainly offers advantages. Grandparents, (who may or may not be the homeowner) can assist with meal preparation and childcare which can facilitate the ability of both spouses to pursue paid employment outside of the home. And larger families living under one roof provide a base level of social interaction and ward off the isolation of singles living. This is no small matter in an era where a U.S. study found that 25 percent of Americans claim to have no close friends[i]. It is also reasonable to conclude that the pressures on the ownership and rental markets would be much worse in our largest cities if even more people pursued independent living.

Extended family living has some drawbacks. Today's modern subdivisions generally have narrow roadways and sidewalks on one side only and are not designed for households with three, four, and even five vehicles. The number of vehicles in some suburban neighbourhoods can cause problems on holidays, garbage-pick-up days, and snow days.

The COVID-19 pandemic has revealed an unanticipated benefit of extended family households. Seniors who might otherwise be living independently in apartments, retirement homes, or care facilities but who instead live with family have relieved the health care system of a significant additional patient load in Canada's most at-risk population. Many Canadians will not soon forget the heartache of losing a loved one to the virus and being unable to visit their retirement residence because of the lockdown. How much better off these seniors would have been living with family in a smaller grouping and where protection from the virus would have been much easier.

The Covid-19 pandemic will change Canada's housing market in ways not yet fully understood. Many office workers will end up working remotely from home permanently, freeing them to live a considerable distance from their employer in smaller communities with cheaper housing while no longer having to face a long daily commute.

While work-from-home solutions may be temporary for some, a new-found importance of home may emerge as a more permanent consideration for buyers. The dangers of the pandemic — such as relying on daycare or navigating the grocery store — may translate into buyers who want to create a self-contained family unit with a playground and veggie garden. At the same time, the extended family seems to have proven its worth and could be supported and encouraged through tax incentives and more innovative home design: perhaps the duplex with a full basement should make a re-appearance in our housing inventory.

2.11: The Christmas Tree

The holidays will soon be upon us and seemingly every year issues and questions arise related to the season's religious and cultural icons and practices.

Whither the Christmas tree?

Some believe that the Christmas tree represents a blend of pagan beliefs or worship with Christian beliefs. But it would be more accurate to say that any pagan origins and meanings have been supplanted by Christian beliefs. Part of the genius of the church was that it infused new, Christian meanings into once pagan, but beloved, holidays and practices.

Whatever meaning the tree may have once had, the fact is that it no longer has that meaning but has become part of the celebration of Christ's birth. It just doesn't matter what it may have once meant to other people centuries ago but no longer means today. And now, many of our fellow citizens of various faiths and beliefs have adopted the tree as a sort of generic symbol of peace and goodwill.

So, to my fellow Christians (and everyone else), enjoy your tree with your family and have a merry (and meaningful) holiday season.

Chapter 3

RACE AND MINORITIES

3.1 Black Lives Matter: Why are people protesting?

Are the anti-Black racism protestors just preaching to the choir?

We are told that "Black Lives Matter". To my knowledge, no one has disputed this although many prefer the slogan be broadened to "All Lives Matter".

Protestors march holding signs which read "No Justice No Peace". Again, no one has a problem with this at all. In the George Floyd case, the offending police officer was fired immediately and charged with murder. Other officers at the scene have since been charged as well. Isn't this how the judicial system is supposed to work?

North America is a huge geographic area with a population of almost 400 million. Outrageous things happen everyday. It would be quite easy to review the print and electronic media daily and cherry-pick disturbing news items (e.g., racial anti-Semitism, vandalism and graffiti on mosques, abuse, and fraud against senior citizens etc.) and conflate these incidents as evidence of a wider "systemic" problem which requires new government initiatives and interventions.

There are quality-of-life deficits among black populations, but they are there because the institutions of the larger society are delinquent in sequestering the hoodlums and incorrigibles who live among impecunious working-class blacks.

Forget life in the hood: young black males are more likely to die installing solar panels than via interactions with the police.

There is little evidence of widespread racial bias, abuse of power, or excessive use of force among police officers nationwide or that identifiable groups are unfairly targeted. Let's stop pretending that there is.

3.2 The Advancement of Minorities

The liberal media seems to have as its task the continual stirring of the pot to keep racialized minorities in a state of anger by constantly reprising everything bad that has ever happened. Yet people like Ronald McNair, the Black astronaut killed in the Challenger disaster, are rarely mentioned. The media wants minorities to be angry over something and to keep them that way.

People who constantly stoke conflict and division are destroying North American society and playing with fire. They are creating a society of tribes that compete for ever-dwindling resources in a dirty zero-sum game that is fought out in the court room, in the lobbyist's office and in the court of public opinion.

A whole industry has grown up in North America comprising diversity consultants, administrators, and various outside activist groups, all of whom have a vested interest in heightening racial and sexual grievances for the simple reason that they make a living from such things. These progressive leftists conceal their will to power underneath bromides about "making a better world".

The progressive left has instantiated what has been termed the *Pyramid of Victims*. At the top are Blacks and at the bottom conservative, Christian, straight, white men and women. Other levels include the LGBTQ+ community, Muslims, Hispanics, liberal women, and so on. Rankings are adjusted based on the offense of the day (*infraction du jour* in Quebec). The lower a group is on the pyramid, the more they can be libeled, slandered, insulted and attacked with impunity. For four years Donald Trump was on the bottom of the bottom. Anyone could say anything about him with zero repercussions.

But who wants to live in a place where people are constantly at each other's throats, where there is never peace because everyone thinks other tribes have an unfair advantage at their own tribe's expense?

The rifts in our society are already deep and there is no shortage of extremely angry people with massive chips on their shoulders.

3.3 Racism

The liberal left has a deep and abiding faith in anti-racist education. Racism, they believe, is always rooted in irrational prejudices or is the poisonous legacy of a troubled upbringing. It is unrelated to the reality of everyday life and never the product of rational thought. They're wrong.

God may have perfect knowledge of all things, but human beings don't. Modern man is an evolutionary creature whose ancestors survived for thousands of years by making judgements with imperfect information: that rustling sound in the treeline was probably just the wind but could be a crouching predator, so better make a detour. Many unnecessary detours were made but caution kept people alive.

Fast-forward to 2019. The past year or so in Greater Toronto has witnessed handgun murders in bars, restaurants, hotels, private homes, apartments, parking lots, and in vehicles on local streets and highways. Two murders even occurred at teenage after-prom parties, one in Peel and the other in York Region. In almost every instance the accused or the victims are racialized minorities.

With gunplay a seemingly daily occurrence, do people develop fears, phobias, and prejudices against identifiable groups? Of course they do, it would be surprising if they didn't. Racism may be wrong, but it is not completely irrational.

Law-abiding Canadians don't need more sensitivity training or anti-racism hectoring. They need people to behave better.

3.4 Anti-Black racism

We are all the same under the skin, but we are culturally different. Diversity is not about skin color; it is about culture, except, of course, when it is not, like when black people show black pride. But black people (and others) would not have to notice their own race – and thus be proud of it – if white people would stop noticing people's skin color.

Because, you see, race does not really exist, but racism does because white people will not stop looking at race and that is terrible, but it's OK for blacks and others to notice race because they must because white people won't stop noticing it.

If white people would just stop noticing people's skin color, racism would end and therefore racial differences would end, and we would all be happy. But white people will not stop because they are evil Nazis who want to keep people down to prop themselves up.

It's an interesting tautology. Racial differences are caused by racism. What's your proof that racism causes racial difference? Answer: Racial differences. Eliminate racism and you end racial differences. Since only whites can be racist if racial difference keeps showing up, that means that whites continue to be racist. At some point, the Looney Left will tire of waiting for racist whites to stop being racist so the logic will change from "eliminate racism and you eliminate racial differences" to "eliminate white people and you eliminate racial differences."

It's implied that anyone can teach white, Asian, or Hispanic students but only blacks can teach other blacks because black teachers can see black students in a way that's untarnished by the stereotypes. Of course, this stereotypes non-black teachers as tarnished with biases, which is racist.

As they said in the 1960's, can you dig it?

3.5 Who will want to teach in Peel?

Peel residents are likely aware of the turmoil at the Peel District School Board over the past several years.

Conflict has centered on systemic discrimination, specifically anti-Black racism; human resources practices; board leadership; and governance issues.

In late June 2020, Ontario's Education Minister terminated the board's Director of Education, having concluded that he did not have the ability to carry out effectively his responsibilities to oversee and ensure proper compliance with the Ministry directions to the Peel board dealing with these issues.

Among other things, the PDSB is tasked with developing an action plan to "address and eliminate statistically significant disproportionalities in enrolment, achievement and outcomes of Black students" in all programs.

And all suspensions and expulsions of students in junior kindergarten and senior kindergarten must cease as of September 2021, and of students in Grades 1 to 3 as of September 2022.

Finally, "statistically significant racial disparities" in all in-school and out-of-school suspensions, exclusions, and expulsions must be eliminated by September 2021.

What will it be like teaching under this new regime? An optimist would believe that teachers will re-double their efforts and wade into the fray ready and willing to negotiate the landmines.

Good luck with that.

Unfortunately, a much-more-likely scenario would be the following: A white teacher has a talented but troubled Black student with a difficult home life. Rather than going the extra mile with him she instead takes the path of least resistance passing him along to the next grade. She thus avoids tough-love or other quasi-disciplinary measures that might benefit the student but risk blowback in the form of complaints and grievances from parents. And with a militant Human Resources department standing by eager and willing to make an example of someone, who could blame the teacher for her actions?

3.6 Public comments on police 'street check' law

Two things are relevant to the public discussion on street checks or "carding". First, do the new regulations permit the practice as the public understands it and, second, is carding a useful tool for law enforcement in the fight against crime? If the answer is "yes" to both it seems that it should be done.

The concern that some groups are "unfairly targeted" is a weak argument. The most dangerous demographic cohort in Canada is young males (those under the age of 30) who are unmarried and often unemployed. So, by definition, the police are "targeting" some group more than others. Unfortunately, within this cohort are sub-categories of individuals identified by race and ethnicity.

Is this fair? No, probably not. But consider that hundreds of people across the country accused of serious crimes are held in remand and deprived of their liberty for months and even years before their cases come to court. This even though the principle of innocent-until-proven-guilty is at the foundation of our judicial system. What are judges to do? They would be remiss in their duties not to detain accused individuals who are either a flight-risk or pose a threat to the public

Law enforcement and the judicial system: it is what it is. The best way to avoid any of this is to be a law-abiding citizen.

3.7 To Kill a Mockingbird

The idea that *To Kill a Mockingbird* must be read and discussed through a "critical, anti-oppression lens" is absurd and should be roundly condemned by all of us.

Schools are supposed to teach how to think, not what to think. The notion that students and teachers require guidance in advance implies that they cannot be trusted to reach proper conclusions.

The book should be approached in the manner that scholars review religious texts. First, conduct *exegesis*: this involves the careful, systematic study of the book to discover the original, intended meaning as historical readers would have understood it. This is primarily an historical task. This would then be followed by *hermeneutics*, which involves seeking the contemporary relevance of the book, i.e., its meaning and lessons in the "here and now".

But treat the teachers and students as adults and let them decide what the book is about and its relevance for a modern audience.

3.8 Slavery in America

The ancestors of black American slaves were not kings and queens in Africa. They were individuals and tribes who were powerless. They were not "captured" by white dudes in colonial outfits like in Roots. They were systematically captured by more powerful African tribes as commodities to be sold at slave ports and auctions. It was a cynical business transaction that enriched powerful African tribes.

That is not very motivating, energizing or inspiring to Beyoncé/Black Lives Matter etc., nor is it effective for demoralizing, shaming, and intimidating regular Americans. But it is the truth.

The second part of the slavery story is the financiers, middlemen, insurers, underwriters, shipping companies and bookkeepers who arranged, planned, and organized the movement of human cargo across the ocean. The mainstream, progressive liberal media and Hollywood are not much interested in elaborating on this part of the story.

So, we have endless movies, shows and articles about Bubba the plantation owner in Alabama but nothing about the first two parts of the slavery story. And today, even though there are many millions more black people in slavery in Africa and the Arab world than there ever were in America, it is not even acknowledged, much less actively discussed, criticized or fought against.

If the motivation of the media, corporate and cultural masters was to educate and enlighten, they would share the full history and fight against the slavery ongoing today.

3.9 Samuel Opuku

Samuel Opuku is a Ghana-born young man who embarked on a 3-day reign of terror in the City of Toronto between November 22-25, 2019. He attacked students and others at the York University and the University of Toronto campuses, dousing them with fecal matter.

Opuku quickly became the "butt" of many jokes and was variously referred to as the *"Turd Tossing Terrorist"*, the *"Feces-Flinging Foreign Felon"*, and the *"Poop Pitching Pervert."*

Opoku's victims were Asian students who were mostly third year (turd year?) undergraduates.

The shit hit the fan when Opuku was discovered living at the YMCA shelter at Queen and Spadina, in Toronto's historic Chinatown. Responding to a Call of Doodie, and determined to "wipe-out" this menace, officers from 52 Division arrested Opuku and he was charged with five counts of assault with a weapon and five counts of mischief.

Thankfully, Opuku surrendered peacefully and did not have to be "flushed out".

3.10 Is Rap Music a Form of Hate Speech?

It's a distressing thought that Mississauga residents share our city with people who have this incredible idea that if you don't like someone (or their music) it's okay to murder them in cold blood. Nothing chivalrous about it: no gentleman's duel at sunrise. Shoot them in front, or shoot them in the back, and if innocent bystanders are killed or wounded, hey, life happens.

The latest incident in Malton on September 15 was apparently motivated by a rap video. There is so much talk about handgun bans and gun control but perhaps some review should be given to rap music as a form of hate speech. It certainly seems to incite levels of violence comparable to drug dealing, if the murders and mayhem of recent decades in North America are any indication.

3.11 Diversity: Part 1

In common parlance, diversity means three (3) things: 1. male/female sex and male and female gender; 2. Race (i.e., heritable physiological traits); 3. Ethnicity (i.e., culture, customs, and language). These traits, **and only these**, are relevant and interesting and must be reflected in our workforces, our post-secondary education system, and our entertainment.

The problem is that any random group of people is diverse. Every human is unique and whole from birth, our DNA never to be repeated. And we are given a soul by God: we do not need anyone else to complete us.

So, imagine a group of thirty German males, all blond-haired and blue-eyed, and all roughly similar in age if you like. They work at a BMW test facility on advanced systems engineering. Not diverse? Wrong. They would surely differ from one another in a multitude of areas: socio-economic background, religiosity, family life, sexual orientation, political views, moral values, educational backgrounds. temperaments, sensibilities, and hobbies to name a few.

But these differences are not considered interesting. There is no reason – none – to believe that the talent of this group would be enhanced by the introduction of women and minorities **unless** these newcomers possessed greater skills that were both valid and job-related. And if this were true no one would have a problem.

No empirical study exists showing the benefits of diversity, it is all just rationalization (hamster treadmill spinning). In fact, the entire modern world was largely created by a non-diverse group of dead white males living approximately from London to Berlin.

Examine the world's great companies and you will find that, at their founding, diversity wasn't a thought and later on, not even an afterthought. It was just irrelevant. Only when the Al Sharpton's and the Social Justice Warriors (SJW's) showed up did they realize they "needed" diversity.

Historically, creativity has been non-diverse. Great inventions or technical leaps forward come from very non-diverse, uniform, high-trust environments: China for silk, the compass, firearms, gunpowder, paper money, etc. Late 18th Century England for the Steam Engine, late 19th Century America for the telephone, etc. Even the airplane was not invented by "diverse" groups but by a couple of bicycle mechanics from Ohio.

The idea that homogeneous groups are less creative and less insightful than diverse ones is ridiculous. Also ridiculous is that they are more prone to group think and less likely to question faulty assumptions. In fact, racially diverse college and university campuses in North America are the epitome of group think and the epitome of lack of individuality.

Nevertheless, there are compelling reasons for diversity in certain situations. Police Services, for example, value diversity because most criminals prefer to be arrested by someone who looks like them.

In truth, I would like to see more diversity. Let's have more heterosexuals employed in the interior design and fashion industries. And how about Big Tech break down barriers by hiring older people (i.e., over the age of 40) with conservative political views? They certainly could: they're able to convince large numbers of young college-educated females to forgo motherhood and relinquish family and re-locate to expensive cities where they have to live like rats for glorified secretarial jobs. (Oops, I mean "knowledge worker" jobs with fancy job titles.)

University science departments could be more inclusive by hiring people of faith who believe in God and that supernaturalism is a fundamental part of reality.

One can imagine the scene as the first pro-life, Christian physics professor is escorted onto campus with a police escort while angry feminists with blue hair and bolts in their noses scream obscenities. A scene reminiscent of integration at the University of Alabama might unfold, where on May 16, 1963, a federal district court in Alabama ordered the university to admit African American students Vivien Malone and James Hood during its summer session. (Interesting fact: NFL Hall-of-Famer Joe Namath was among the student onlookers that day)

Alabama Governor George Wallace had made a campaign promise a year earlier to prevent the school's integration even if it required that he stand in the schoolhouse door. Who will be this generations Wallace?

Increasing diversity at universities won't be easy. Radical feminists and other SJW's are constantly vigilant for any expression of opinion that could be considered pro-white, pro-Christian, pro-Israel, pro-male or, of course, pro-life.

Any conservative viewpoint that is.

3.12 Diversity: Part 2

Diversity, and its kissing cousin equity, are slippery, malleable words.

"Is it Just Me?"

Sometimes when a group is over-represented in a certain endeavour it's okay. The NBA and the NFL, for example, are about 70 percent black while black males comprise no more than 6-7 percent of the general U.S. population. That's okay, they are there on merit, i.e., talent. But if the corporate boards of large companies (or Nobel laureates) are overwhelmingly white and male that's because of racism, systemic discrimination, and white privilege rooted in patriarchy.

The progressive definition of privilege is having better social and economic outcomes than another group. It can be shown statistically that blacks have poorer social and economic outcomes than whites, and that men (on average) have higher incomes than women. Hence, overall, white men are "privileged" according to modern blank-slate progressive thinking which assumes everyone is biologically equal and has similar life goals.

In Canada, blacks comprise just 3.5 percent of the population but are now in seemingly 90 percent of TV commercials particularly those involving small businesses, automobiles, real estate, or banking. Blacks are portrayed as entrepreneurs, managers, involved in inter-racial relationships, or are seen in monogamous relationships purchasing homes in the suburbs with their high school sweethearts and their 2.1 children. And every television station and talk show has a diversity hire.

(Do advertisers know that most blacks are poor and don't vote?)

The GLBTQ community comprises less than 5 percent of the North American population with gays and lesbians being perhaps 1-2 percent each. That's it. But turn on Netflix and search for lesbian content and the line-up is longer than the queue at a Texas foodbank. A sample: *Elite, The Umbrella Academy, Pose, Wynonna Earp, Tales on the City, Trinkets, She-Ra and the Princesses of Power, One Day at a Time, Glee, Special, Sense 8, Orange is the New Black,*

Everything Sucks, Schitts Creek, Degrassi: Next Class, Chilling Adventures of Sabrina, Feel Good, The Politician, Hollywood, Queer Eye, Gypsy, Sotus The Series, AJ and the Queen, A Queen is Born, and on…and on…and on.

Given the numbers of closeted homosexuals and lesbians during Hollywood's Golden Age and given the number of current day celebrities "coming out" as gay or bi-sexual on a regular basis, it is likely that the LBTGQ+ community was, and is, significantly over-represented in the film and entertainment community. So how did they become a marginalized group?

It is also difficult to make the case that Blacks, and other minorities are under-represented. The entertainment business is bottom-line oriented and casting decisions and scripts are directed solely at producing a marketable product. No one cares whether minorities are represented if the product is entertaining and profitable.

No one really wants to see a female or a Black James Bond either. Ian Fleming's Bond was white, a character of the Cold War, and his era ended in the 1970's. The post-Roger Moore films have little to do with the real Bond, and more recent films nothing at all - - - they're not even based on Ian Fleming novels.

Black actress Viola Davis claims that she is the "Black Meryl Streep" and should be paid equally. She doesn't get. If someone wanted to pay her Streep's rate they would but she's just not as marketable i.e., Streep's films do better at the box office. That's how free enterprise works: let the market determine people's worth.

People like Davis need to stop having their cake and eating it too. If they want to use race to gain special treatment, they need to prove that they are being discriminated against in the first place and that it's not just a fair outcome due to talent, intelligence, or valid business decisions after having received an equal opportunity.

It must be conceded nevertheless that society doesn't have legitimacy if everyone in power is white, rich, and overwhelmingly from elite high schools followed by matriculation from Harvard and Yale. In theory, you get a meritocracy but in reality, you get a country that's run solely for the benefit of those with "merit". And there's a big difference.

Teaching children to appreciate *diversity* but erroneously calling this virtue of open-mindedness *fairness* is wrong. Those two values are so commonly confused that any critique is immediately met with charges of prejudice, discrimination, racism, sexism, and bigotry. But having favorites and having an open mind about differences are not mutually exclusive.

3.13 Be a Better Friend to Career Felons

During the "mostly peaceful" protests and associated violence, looting and arson such as occurred in Democrat-governed states and cities in the summer of 2020, it became apparent just how shabby America's treatment of career felons has been.

Laid bare for all to see was the tired, conservative, "pale-stale-male" approach to policing. Historically, this involved law-abiding citizens (mainly those city residents who work and pay taxes) electing representatives to city council who, in turn, would develop public policy in consultation with senior management. But a far better, more progressive approach was pioneered by New York mayor Bill De Blasio: make decisions dealing with police budget cuts and funding priorities in an authoritarian manner after ad-hoc consultation with protesters and unemployed stoners, (often the same people).

But even if we are not city mayors, elected officials, or even a poet or a folk-singer, there are things that all of us can do today to demonstrate solidarity with career felons:

1. Learn about the history of crime and its contribution to America's greatness.
2. Educate yourself about career felons.
3. Be intolerant of intolerance; if you hear law-abiding citizens speaking in a bigoted manner towards career felons, speak up.
4. Avoid segregation; if career felons are not included in you circle of friends and your social life that's not okay.
5. Speak to your kids; increasingly, children are being taught that career felons are the cause of many societal problems and that current-day and historical career felons should be targets of disapproval.
6. Most importantly, LISTEN when career felons are speaking.

It's up to all of use to make a better society.

Chapter 4

SPORTS

4.1 The Olympic Games: Cancel them for good.

On March 22, 2020, the Canadian Olympic Committee and Canadian Paralympic Committee issued joint statements saying that they refuse to send their teams to Tokyo unless their respective Games are pushed back a year. Two days later the International Olympic Committee and Japanese government agreed to postpone the 2020 Summer Olympics to a date beyond "2020 but not later than summer 2021."

Promising developments but why stop there: just cancel the Games for good.

Rio de Janeiro hosted the last Summer Olympics in 2016 and only lost billions doing it. Doubling down on another large public event, Rio celebrated its annual Carnival in February 2017, and except for the race riots, gang wars, numerous victims, fires, and looting, it was almost fun.

The modern-day Olympics have expanded and mutated to be unrecognizable from their roots and not just because of rampant commercialism and the participation of professionals. Almost anything now qualifies as an "Olympic" event: games (golf); outdoor vacation activities (kayaking, beach volleyball); hobbies (climbing, surfing, sailing.)

No doubt, the Tokyo Olympics will be rife with the obligatory cheating and doping scandals. And Olympic ads are just so smarmy. In addition to the endless virtue signalling around diversity there is the constant, cloying invocation of "dreams"; the flag-waving by multinational companies that do not really care about the country; the incredibly lame metaphors linking the widget industry to bobsledding or whatever; and so on.

The Olympic Games: an idea whose time has gone.

4.2.1 The National Football League: Part 1

College sports in the United States are incredibly corrupt, particularly men's football and basketball. Everyone knows it but pretends not to notice and the issue is quietly avoided.

Each year, America's third-and-fourth tier colleges and universities (and even some of its world-class schools like Duke and the University of Michigan) admit sub-literate hood rats to fill out their football rosters, masquerading as students for a semester or two. They are given athletic scholarships and live gratis in the jock dorms, often dodging felony-rape allegations while cutting classes. (But hey, how are they supposed to know that having sex with a drunk and unconscious co-ed is considered "non-consensual" under the law?)

A lucky handful of these "students" are selected in the National Football League (NFL) draft each year while most others end up with nothing, not even a college degree. Well, they do end up with some things: aching tendons, ligaments and joints, arthritis seeping into their spine and knee joints before the age of forty, excruciating headaches from concussions, and if they're really unlucky, Chronic Traumatic Encephalopathy (CTE) by age fifty. Assuming they are still alive and can walk.

Imagine a hypothetical first-round draft pick, let's call him wide receiver Deleterious Jones. The pro scouts were really high on Deleterious: after his freshman season at Quaker State, he red-shirted for a year before transferring to North-West Louisiana Tech. He was admitted without question at NWLT because he met the school's standards for athletes: he had shoes and teeth.

Deleterious had a break-out senior year with 49 catches, 82 rushes from scrimmage and 2 arrests. The one rap on Deleterious was that, despite years of weightlifting and steroid use (he bench-pressed the team bus at the scouting combine) he often dropped 14-yard passes in the clutch in the red zone. He was a project.

Deleterious, the youngest of ten, arrived on NFL Draft Day with his mother LaQuanteesha and two of his brothers, Dexatrim and Tylenol. He was wearing the obligatory one-size-too-small suit which accentuated the fact that his neck and head circumference were identical. With his orange hair, bolt in his nose, and gang tattoos covering his entire body, Deleterious knew that he would fit in with the other NFL players. Already, he was "building his brand".

The Commissioner announced: *"With the third pick overall, the Florida Felons select Deleterious Jones, wide receiver, North-West Louisiana Tech."*

Florida thought Deleterious would fit into their offence as a deep-threat to take the heat off of its young and promising backfield comprising halfback DeeFelon Williams and fullback LaThuggy Brown. They also planned to use Deleterious and DeeFelon for kick-off returns.

You can imagine the first kick-off return of the season with former NBC sportscaster Dick Enberg calling the play:

"Oh my, what a year this young man has had."

"Jones and Williams set to receive and there's the kick"

"Jones fields the ball at his 20-yard line."

"Jones breaks one tackle and returns the ball to the 30…the 35..the..40."

"OH MY, HE's BEEN SHOT!!!.......DELETERIOUS HAS BEEN SHOT!!"

"SOMETHING HAS HAPPENED IN THE MOTORCADE ROUTE"*

(*A shout-out to older readers who remember the Kennedy Assassination).

4.2.2 The National Football League: Part 2

I think that I speak for all NFL fans when I say how much I admire the ghetto athletes that have populated NFL rosters the last twenty-plus years or so.

The self-effacing, quiet dignity with which they play the game and respect its traditions. Consummate team players committed to winning and so loath to draw attention to themselves.

And I love the clothes they wear --- over-size sunglasses, over-size headphones, and suits that rodeo clowns wouldn't be caught dead in.

Since many modern-day players began to take to the field in a steroid-induced rage, games began to drag on in order to accommodate the venting required. This included the end-zone dances

"Is it Just Me?"

(remember Elbert "Ickey" Woods and the Ickey Shuffle?), the ball-spiking, the trash-talking, the touchdown-mobbing, the jumping into the end-zone stands (very popular in Green Bay), the high-fives, the chest-beating and the "Aww-right" fist pump to name a few.

Now of course, extra time is required for pre-game kneeling in order to disrespect veterans, the American flag and America's men-and-women serving in the military. This is done to advance the cause of justice for career felons such as George Floyd (not to be confused with former British Prime Minister Lloyd George.)

It didn't help that the broadcast and print media rarely called out unsportsmanlike conduct. The worst offenders were routinely described as "misunderstood" or even "colorful."

****

It is tempting to point the finger at Black players from low-income neighbourhoods and "the projects" as the cause of so much of the bad behavior and show-boating in the NFL in recent years but this is far from an entirely satisfactory explanation.

Blacks have played in the league for decades and none of them ever behaved in the manner we commonly witness today. Go down the list: Bobby Mitchell, Jim Brown, Night Train Lane, Emlen Tunnell, Lenny Moore, Lem Barney, Mel Farr, Paul Warfield, and many, many others. When Jim Brown scored a touchdown, he just flipped the ball to the referee and made his way to the Cleveland bench.

My best guess is that bad behavior in the NFL simply reflects the "me-first" attitude of recent generations who have been raised to hold hedonism above all. Whatever feels good goes. Freedoms and rights are things for legislators and judges to conjure out of thin air, not precious traditions forged in the crucible of history.

As a rough parallel, in the first few centuries after the establishment of Christianity, artists, sculptors, and painters commonly dedicated their efforts to the glory of God and thus left their works unsigned. As history unfolded, ego crept in and artists began to sign their works.

4.2.3 The National Football League: Part 3

What the heck happened with Super Bowl halftime shows? They used to be somewhat corny, but they were fun and reflected the best of American exceptionalism.

The first seven years, 1967-74 featured primarily marching bands from colleges and universities, with the exception of Carol Channing in 1970. There were military themes as well, including a re-enactment of the Battle of New Orleans in 1970 and the USMC tattoo in 1972. Later years saw wonderful tributes to artists such as Louis Armstrong, Duke Ellington, and eras including the Big Band Era, and Motown.

These were the good years of family entertainment, where everyone could watch, and your impulse was not to send young kids out of the room.

Later years, very hit-or-miss, notable stinkers include the Black-Eyed Peas (2011) and Maroon 5 (2019) And whose idea was it to have Beyonce in both 2013 and 2016, the latter year in which she came out in a leather bathing suit, and with her back-up dancers and a scowl on her face tromped around protesting something-or-other? The 2020 halftime show was even worse, with a couple of middle-age women pole-dancing (Shakira and Jennifer Lopez) dressed in bustiers.

Great family entertainment.

Today's music is not that great anyway, to put it mildly. The music video with the obligatory aerobics-workout back-up dancers has been done to death. Otherwise, it's boring and overdone, the artists themselves pretentious, scripted, choreographed, lip-synced, auto-tuned and contrived, who change their public image every other week. They are not real musicians; they are just marketing schemes. Their four-tone "music" is barfed out mostly by some computer programmer in Sweden apparently.

Rappers murder each other on a regular basis but White Supremacists, who do next to nothing, are the problem.

Popular music today just misses the whole point of youth, testosterone, estrogen, and rebelliousness. The great bands like Bachman-Turner Overdrive, Motley Crew, Van Halen, and Alice Cooper got their start in their parent's garage and built a local following playing small venues, high school dances and bars. They weren't "discovered" at a shopping mall in Orlando. Vince Neil, Randy Bachman, Alice Cooper, and the Van Halen brothers were the smart-ass kids you went to high school with, who smoked (everything), made you laugh, dissed the teacher behind his back, and cut classes. They were real people, and their music was real. And that's why we loved them.

4.2.4 The National Football League: Part 4

Who is the NFL's all-time number one felon?

Aaron Hernandez and O.J. Simpson immediately spring to mind but it's not that simple. The League has employed a prodigious amount of criminal talent over the years so narrowing-down to the best-of-the-best is not easy.

But who would be the one player who could end the argument, the "go-to" guy who would cause a moment of silence and nodding agreement among patrons in even the most intense of bar room debates? Answer: Lawrence Phillips.

Phillips was the Bomb: an all-around felon who was as comfortable with domestic assault and murder as he was with vandalism, receiving bribes and committing suicide. A phenom in league with Wayne Gretzky and Tiger Woods.

Consider these stats from Phillip's Wikipedia page:

Item: Less than two weeks after helping the University of Nebraska win the 1994 national championship, his sophomore year, Phillips pleaded not guilty to charges of assault, vandalism, and disturbing the peace. The charges came from a March 1994 incident, in which Phillips was accused of grabbing a 21-year-old college student "around the neck". Phillips had earlier entered into a pretrial diversion program, but was charged on November 18, 1994, after failing to complete the requirements of the program.

Item: Shortly before the start of the 1995 season, Phillips' eligibility was in question for receiving a $100 lunch from a sports agent during the 1994 season.

Item: Hours after the team returned from East Lansing on September 10, 1995, Phillips assaulted his ex-girlfriend, basketball player Kate McEwen. He dragged McEwen out of her apartment by the hair and down three flights of stairs before smashing her head into a mailbox.

Item: After being released by the St Louis Rams, his draft team, Phillips lasted two games in Miami in 1996, but the Dolphins released him after he pleaded no contest to assaulting a woman in a Plantation, Florida nightclub.

Item: The year 2005 was a banner year for Phillips. On August 21, 2005, he was arrested for assault after driving a car into three teenagers following a dispute with them during a pick-up football game in Los Angeles, California. At the time of the arrest, Phillips was also wanted by the San Diego Police Department in connection with two alleged domestic-abuse incidents involving a former girlfriend who claimed that Phillips had choked her to the point of unconsciousness. In addition, the Los Angeles Police Department was seeking Phillips in connection with another allegation of domestic abuse that had occurred in Los Angeles. In March 2006, Phillips was ordered to stand trial on charges of felony assault with a deadly weapon stemming from the August 21, 2005, incident.

Item: On October 10, 2006, Phillips was found guilty on seven counts. On October 3, 2008, he was sentenced to 10 years in a California state prison.

Item: Phillips wasn't finished: On April 12, 2015, his cellmate, Damion Soward, was found dead in the cell the two men shared. Phillips was regarded as the prime suspect in the case and on September 1, 2015, he was charged with first-degree murder in Soward's death.

Item: Phillips was awaiting trial in segregated custody when he was found unresponsive in his cell by correctional officers around midnight on January 12, 2016. A coroner determined that he had hanged himself in prison.

So, multiple assault charges, a murder, and a suicide. Forget about it.

Take that O.J.

POSTSCRIPT:

Aside from an enviable criminal record, Lawrence Phillips is notable for a number of interesting football-related events.

At the 1996 NFL Draft he was widely expected to be selected by the new Baltimore Ravens with the fourth pick to fill their vacant running back position. However, Baltimore decided to take the best available player regardless of position, and with the fourth pick they selected offensive tackle (and future Hall of Famer) Jonathan Ogden. Ravens General Manager Ozzie Newsome in fact went against the wishes of the team's owner and most of his scouts in selecting Ogden. They all wanted Phillips. Newsome settled on Ogden once he was comfortable that Ogden could play guard rather than the tackle position he had played in college.

Phillips ended up being drafted sixth overall by the St. Louis Rams. The Rams thought so highly of Phillips that on the same day of the draft, they traded his predecessor, Jerome Bettis, to the Pittsburgh Steelers. Bettis went on to play nine seasons with the Steelers, becoming a six-time Pro Bowler and two-time first team All-Pro. He was a member of the Steeler's Super Bowl winning team in 2005.

Last but not least, now playing with The San Francisco 49er's during the 1999 season, in a Monday Night Football game against the Arizona Cardinals, cornerback Aeneas Williams rushed in on a blitz and Phillips failed to pick him up and block him.

Williams ended up knocking future Hall of Fame quarterback Steve Young unconscious on the play with a hard, but clean, hit. Young suffered what would prove to be a career-ending concussion; he did not play again for the rest of the season and was all but forced to retire.

"Is it Just Me?"

4.3 Membership Meeting – Augusta National Golf Club

Chapter 5

RELATIONSHIPS

5.1 Do not Marry the Wrong Person

Yeah, right.

Everybody marries the wrong person: there is no "right" person for **anyone** despite what the YouTube videos and relationship counsellors would have you believe. If you cannot accept this, you cannot be married.

Regardless of who you marry you will go through the same struggles and step on the same landmines as everyone else. How do we know this is true? Because in the United States the divorce rate for second marriages (60 percent) and third marriages (73 percent) are both higher than first marriages (50 percent). If people learned their lessons during their first marriages and married the "right" person next time, the rates for subsequent marriages should be lower not higher. But they are not.

"Is it Just Me?"

Successful marriages can be described with a 2-circle Venn diagram:

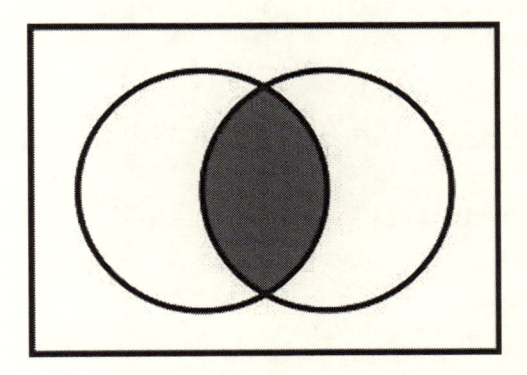

The part that overlaps (the red zone) represents the things that make the relationship work and hold it together: these could be, for example, religion, children, love of travel, basic respect. Everything outside the overlap are the things that pull you apart. So, the key to a marriage that survives is to nurture the overlap. In this example, the degree of overlap is enough to sustain the relationship.

Christians have a ready explanation for the unavoidable difficulties of married life, and indeed life in general. The explanation lies in the fact that God ordained that both the natural world and human beings possess free will. The vagaries of the natural world result in forest fires, floods, hurricanes, tidal waves, and heat waves to name a few. The freedom that humans enjoy allows for moral evil and that good things happen to bad people and bad things happen to good people. This combination of natural world evil and the potential for moral evil ensures that life is often a battle for everyone regardless of wealth, education, or social position. Many relationships, unfortunately, cannot endure life's struggles.

Every human is unique and whole from birth, our DNA never to be repeated. And we are given a soul by God: we do not need anyone else to complete us.

5.2 What does it mean do be "in a relationship"?

What does it mean do be "in a relationship"? The obvious meaning is that a person is dating another person exclusively i.e., monogamy and neither party is seeing anyone else.

But does it mean anything more? It seems to me that for a relationship to succeed it cannot be aimless and just unfold --- there must be a plan or an "endgame" that both parties at least tacitly agree to, otherwise failure is just a matter of time. You must want the same things right from the start.

So, for example, a man and a woman might both want 2 children, a dog, a small home in the country with a white picket fence, and that one partner quit their job and be a stay-at-home- parent until the eldest child is ten. This is an actual plan.

There are only two (2) ways a relationship proceeds: either the parties' break-up or they get married. Nobody stays in a dating relationship for 40 years.

5.3 Open Relationships

Welcome to another invention of the Looney Left.

In a romantic context, a relationship is generally defined something like "an emotional and sexual association between two people." So, when a woman tells a man that she is "seeing someone" or is "in a relationship" it means she is with this person exclusively, i.e., not available for dating from prospective suitors.

By definition therefore, a relationship is closed. An open relationship is a contradiction, like a "square circle" or a "married bachelor."

If a person is involved with more than one other person, there is a term for this. It's called "dating".

And it never occurs to the open-relationship, hook-up, and casual-sex enthusiasts that if these activities gained wide-spread acceptance, why on earth would any sane man or woman remain monogamous and have any desire to marry?

Relationships require rules. No rules, no relationships.

The single best piece of advice for men interested in marriage and family (assuming such a creature still exists) is probably this: don't have sex with a woman you did not marry.

Just as women having sex with random men open the former up to all kinds of possible dangers and abuses (mostly physical), so do men who have sex with random women increase their exposure to the mentally unstable and/or malicious, and the associated risks.

Men and women courted in the old days for a reason. Even if dating couples couldn't wait until marriage, the courtship process involved at least getting to know one's prospective sexual partner for a while and understanding that knowledge of a person's character ought to precede, not follow, physically intimate acts.

Society cannot eat its cake and have it too. We cannot blame women for their sexual promiscuity leading to dangers while exempting men from similar (but somewhat different) risks.

5.4 Stop trying to make women like you.

Every man has undoubtedly done this at some point.

From that first instance of puppy love when we experience the unrequited love of that girl on the other side of the classroom, we imagine that fawning over her would be the key to unlock her heart. Later, when we're older and chasing real women, we employ the same technique: being unfailingly polite and agreeable; calling her often; surprising her with small gifts; bringing her coffee and donuts at work and so on.

Men approach the problem as they might if they struggle with English or Math: get remedial help from a tutor or simply work harder. So, they make even greater efforts to please a girl, believing that they can win her over if they work harder to demonstrate their good qualities.

But chasing very rarely, if ever, works. Why?

One reason of course is that the girl simply doesn't find you appealing or is not interested in a relationship. She may indeed be telling the truth when she rejects you. But men don't get it: their pursuit of her is just an act of selfishness on their part.

Chasing makes the pursuer look needy, desperate, and weak, not qualities most women find attractive. It also creates a superior-subordinate relationship because the woman now feels beholden to someone and if she can't reciprocate the small gifts because of her financial situation she is reminded of her low status. And woman imagine that the man views his small acts of kindness as akin to accumulating Air Miles: one hundred miles gets one date, two hundred miles gets two dates, one thousand miles and she has to marry you.

Don't chase after women guys - - it's not going anywhere.

5.5 Young Men and Marriage

Many young men these days are little-more than life-support systems for video games and cell phones.

"Is it Just Me?"

They can be seen everywhere, hunched over a cellphone with a blank, sullen look on their face. They never met a chair they didn't like.

When tired of sitting at home watching YouTube, Netflix, and porn, they drive their tinted-window Audi/BMW's to the local plaza or mall parking lot after business hours, where they sit, occasionally meeting up with their like-minded friends.

They live in their parent's basement and their wardrobe consists of a basic five-piece, suitable-for-all-occasions attire: sneakers, track pants, t-shirt, hoodie, and backward-facing ball cap. ("C'mon mom leave me alone - - I'll look for a job later. I'm only 29")

They hate dating, let alone marriage and children. Dating requires that they constitute themselves as adults, go out and talk with real women and feign interest in their lives. But what really annoys young men is that dating keeps them away from their one true love: their phone.

You can observe them on dates in restaurants, squirming anxiously in their seats, tiny beads of perspiration forming on their upper lips. Finally, the girl excuses herself to powder her nose and they strike, whipping out the phone at lightening speed, instantly thumbing through texts, e-mails, and social media "likes". (In all fairness, the girl is likely doing the same thing in the powder room.)

They calm down immediately, the way smokers jonesing for a cigarette feel after lighting up.

Millennial men, and now Generation Z, reject the nuclear family, and the religious values that Western culture was built on because they resemble some sort of "unenlightened" old world of responsibility and duty that they want no part of. They have little intellectual curiosity whether they serve a greater social purpose and are more likely to ask if they are happy. They shun values such as marriage, family, self-sacrifice and duty as the pitfalls of suckers and give little thought to the perpetuation of their lineage and culture.

It's a more difficult and intense world now. Young men are learning that it's best, socially and economically, to travel light.

As for sex and romance, with the widespread availability of massage parlors, escort agencies, porn, inflatable women, casual sex, and hook-up dating apps, a man's physical needs can be met quite easily. And the girl is not there the next morning.

****

However, all cynicism aside, I am optimistic for the future and future generations because deep down I think we know that what Western society has done in recent decades is not empowering. Abandoning the guidance of our past and embracing hedonism and subjectivity was not some genius idea. Dismissing the foundations built for us over thousands of years in the form of gender roles, traditional lifestyles, hard work, objectivity, and cultural respect has been, in fact, painfully stupid.

Because really, what have we got to show for it? Nothing but infinite license to put who and what we want in our bodies, while our freedoms to speak, to think, to dream, and to build get more limited every day

We can and must do better. It won't be easy for us to dig ourselves out of the pit that the left-wing indoctrination and mainstream media machines has dug for us, but it's work worth doing.

Chapter 6

ENTERTAINMENT

6.1 Sex and the City – The TV Show

Sex and the City ran on HBO for six seasons from 1998-2004. It was arguably the most annoying television show ever created.

The show featured four female friends living in New York City and centered around the merry mix-ups of their dating and social lives.

The characters all were played by ostensibly heterosexual women, but the show was actually about gay males. The women even had gay occupations: e.g., museum curator, public relations consultant. This allowed them to behave as gays (promiscuous, obsessed with their sexuality, love of fashion) while being politically correct, since gays at that time were protected like Faberge eggs.

All four characters are completely self-absorbed (the gay stereotype) and love getting together on the telephone or in fern bars to commiserate about their "issues", complain about their relationships and, of course, the lack of high-quality men. Yawn.

Although the women are all in their mid-thirties, (Miranda is in her 40's) nevertheless there is no shortage of men interested in dating them even though they (the men) are, of course, mostly unsuitable.

Since women hit their peak SMV (Sexual Market Value) at age 25 (The Wall) and since their fertility peaks at age 28, the idea that high-value men would pursue any of these women is laughable.

Women in their mid-thirties attract men 40-50 who are generally divorced with kids and have lots of baggage. Men in their 30's want women who are 21, not women in their 30's who hit the Wall without an airbag.

6.2 How to be a Female Stand-up Comic

First, make a list of every swear word you can think of in the English language. Don't forget those compound words! See Wong, Ali or Silverman, Sarah if you need mentoring.

Second, think of every gross bodily function you can, preferably related to sexual activity. For example, "sperm" or "eat shit" or "poopy diaper" or "sexual intercourse while menstruating" or "poo-poo on your pee-pee" or "braiding your pubic hair". You get the idea. Use your imagination.

If you are a lesbian, regale the audience with stories about your partner-of-the-week.

If straight, make disparaging references about the sexual performance of your husband or boyfriend. Spare no one even if they are public figures because nothing brings partners closer than public embarrassment.

Take the swear words and mix them up with the gross bodily functions. Rinse and repeat. Make your routine so juvenile and off-putting that sailors get up and walk out. Join men in the race to the bottom.

Congratulations, you are now a female comic! And don't listen to other people's opinions: everyone knows there's nothing more appealing than a middle-age woman with a potty mouth.

6.3 Hollywood and the #MeToo Movement

The #MeToo movement is a social movement fighting sexual abuse and sexual harassment where people publicize allegations of sexual misconduct.

The movement centers around women reporting unwanted and inappropriate sexual advances and demeaning behaviour. It requires men to call out such behaviour when they see it and take a stand against behavior that objectifies women. Men should talk to each other about consent and listen to victims when they tell their stories.

The #MeToo movement came to widespread prominence in October 2017 following the sexual abuse allegations against Miramax Pictures co-founder Harvey Weinstein. An initial Twitter post by actress Alyssa Milano was followed by a number of high-profile posts and responses by her fellow actresses including Gwyneth Paltrow, Ashley Judd, Jennifer Lawrence, and Uma Thurman, among others.

Sexual promiscuity is okay, however. Women in the entertainment industry (when they're not in rehab) can serially date, hook-up, have affairs, have multiple breakups and multiple marriages, perform on stage in leather bathing suits or lingerie, and broaden their sexual identities to include both men and women.

But don't dare assume they are easy and approach them with cheap come-ons. They resent men who do that ---- unless of course the men are rich, famous, good-looking or can help their career. Then it's okay.

How many of the "#MeToo" crowd who invoked righteous indignation over alleged sexual offenses against women are the same people who gave Roman Polanski a pass? We were told that, when it came to Polanski (and any number of others), personal moral failings are no reason not to recognize and celebrate the accomplishments of one who is a talented artist. We must separate the flawed man from the brilliant artist. (And the silence of various people in the entertainment industry probably did have real-world effects on the number of women who were harassed or assaulted but let's not dwell on that).

Apparently, Hollywood is sleazy. Who knew?

The Hollywood women didn't get it. The sorting machine that made them famous is largely arbitrary. There are many more attractive, talented women who want to be in the movies than there are roles available That's the beauty of it. That's why they should feel so grateful if they are among the chosen.

Anyone can be an actor. The single most important qualification is nepotism but if you don't happen to be the offspring of a famous actor, producer, or director then the casting couch might be your only hope. How badly do you want it?

Those who succeed are eternally grateful to Stanford or University of Toronto Medical School or the San Francisco Ballet or whoever allowed them to succeed, especially because they know there were many just as good as they were who were rejected.

And that is why the Hollywood women know (or should know) that if you get out of line (or don't go along to get along) there are plenty of well-qualified people that can be chosen to replace you. So, the physicians keep quiet about scandals in their midst. And the middle managers. And the Hollywood starlets. And the U.S. gymnastics team.

Because they all know they can be replaced in a short time by some "loser" who is just about as good as they are. The chosen ones often don't really deserve it any more than those not chosen, and so the chosen better get with the program.

Ladies, if you want to work with nice people join the Peace Corps.

6.4 Late-Night Talk Shows

I haven't liked late night talk shows since Johnny Carson was the host of the Tonight Show and his last show was May 22, 1992. His replacement, Jay Leno, was okay but he didn't have Carson's boyish charm and intellectual curiosity, so the show and guests weren't as stimulating.

I have no idea who watches any of these shows today: must be a lot of unemployed people and insomniacs. Outrageously repetitive, instead of enlightenment and entertainment they're now just vehicles for interviewing useless celebrities and attacking President Trump, mostly the latter. You don't like him: **WE GET IT**. But just once, it would be nice for Jimmy, Jimmy, Seth, and Stephen et. al., to explain in detail why the Democrats are a much-preferred alternative. Joe Biden: that's who America needs? Really?

Random thoughts:

Trevor Noah: If only he was as funny and as talented as he thinks he is.

Jimmy Fallon: Reminds me of someone's annoying kid brother who always wanted to be cool and hang around the big kids. Finally landed his dream job - - talk show host and celebrity bootlicker.

Ellen DeGeneres: What a scamp, she's just a delight. Not a late-night host but she could be - - - she's that talented! A while back Jason Momora was a guest on her show, and he came on impersonating Elvis Presley. What a fresh, original concept!

Lilly Singh: About as funny as stomach cancer. As a Canadian I apologize.

At the end of their so-called workday these people with their economically meaningless jobs retreat to their homes in Santa Monica, Malibu, Montecito etc., and, to cover their vacuity and triviality, have these fantasies that they are a part of the new "creative economy". In fact. none of them would know what innovation was if they tripped over it. They certainly would not know what honest labor was.

The problems of everyday Americans don't affect them as they wrap themselves in a safe cocoon of wealth and celebrity, never having to deal with anything real. Neither they, nor their children, will ever find themselves at the sharp end of a shooting war in the Middle East, and they don't have to worry about the minimum wage or college tuition fees.

And so, on beautiful sunny days in southern California they drive past miles of homeless encampments in downtown Los Angeles to attend climate change protests. Afterwards, they head home to their gated communities to finish their opinion piece for a women's magazine "Why Trump's Border Wall is a bad idea"

6.5 Celebrities "Sharing"

Celebrities love to share. Not their money of course, but pictures. They love to show you how much better their lives are than yours, all the while acting like they are doing you a favor. It's beautiful: they can be seen as charitable and generous and win the gratitude of the public, all the while feeding their enormous egos at zero cost to themselves. This is one of the worst features of contemporary America: the rich and the few flaunting their wealth and rubbing it in the noses of the poor and the many. So much for *noblesse oblige*.

So, we finally get a tour of Oprah's mansion while Live! With Kelly and Ryan host Kelly Ripa shares Instagram's of her daughter's high school graduation. Other celebs regale us with so-called "Aw-Gee" photos of them at the park with their adorable brats. We're supposed to be edified to know that underneath their fame and fortune celebrities are just like us. Right down to their high school diplomas.

Celebrities like to go on talk shows and discuss their "issues". They are welcome on all shows as long as they are willing to attack Donald Trump. Most are able to summon the courage to do so.

Diseases like anorexia nervosa and bulimia become interesting and fashionable only when celebrities suffer from them. Otherwise, an anorexic is just a skinny kid with a behavioural problem.

6.6 YouTubers

It is no coincidence that Los Angeles became the Mecca of YouTubers.

Whether LA was/is good or bad, it eventually became bad for the United States, with its auto-mania, cultural vapidity, crassness, vulgarity, and shallow narcissism. This basically describes YouTube in 2021.

Los Angeles may no longer be what it used to be, although you can see evidence of *Los Angelesization* all over the nation and even around the world, in places like Dubai and Shanghai. A neo-urban planning of pure artifice and without roots and identity. Plaster/plastic cities.

YouTube embodies the worst of "Social Media" in substituting for real-life social interaction. Close behind are all the entertainment options (IPODs, smartphones, video games, DVDs, satellite TV) that make it easy to kill time without being in the vicinity of other human beings.

YouTube used to feature a charming, rustic collection of guitar lessons, collectors and hobbyists, home handymen, magicians, lecturers, moms in the kitchen etc. Now it's basically a toxic, soft-porn site overrun by Kardashian/Jenner-wannabees who are willing to say anything, do anything or confess anything (e.g., "how many people have you slept with --- relatives don't count") for their fifteen minutes of fame.

Welcome to the culture of the gutter.

Loudness and vulgarity are now spun as "edgy" and "keeping it real". Being obnoxious makes you "chill" and breathtaking amounts of self-promotion and self-absorption is considered admirable. Hey, you're "building your brand."

The United States has millions of young women who suffer from bi-polar disorder, Attention Deficit Disorder (ADD), autism, anxiety and depression, low self-esteem and Attention Deficit Hyperactivity Disorder (ADHD). Seemingly every one of them has a YouTube site, and the obligatory Twitter and Instagram feed.

Tune in to the endless channels offering fashion tips, make-up tips, jewelry tips, relationship advice etc. and you will witness enormous amounts of hair-flinging, earring twirling, perpetual giggling, swearing, drinking, and mile-a-minute marginally coherent run-on sentences punctuated by the phrase "I'm like" every other word.

And, of course, even otherwise sweet young women, if they want to build views on their channel, must succumb to answering personal questions about their sexuality, hook-ups, loss of virginity, drug use, cheating, weight gain etc. Hence, the inevitable "tell all" video appears within a year or two of establishing themselves. Years ago, (when people had class and were better behaved), these were private matters. Women had regard for their self-worth, dignity and would avoid embarrassing their families.

Alas, we're not in Kansas anymore.

YouTubers are supposed to be edifying and educational but they're not. Most are trivial, repetitive, boring and pointless.

YouTube reflects the worst features of contemporary America and the Western world in general: social atomization, competition, status anxiety, financial insecurity, and smartphone usage. Everybody has an amazing Instagram/Facebook profile online, but they struggle in real life.

Social media has given us an abundance of imaginary, on-line friends but few real ones. We have learned to live in the moment, with no expectations, happy to have a glimpse of intimacy from time to time.

Loneliness is now the human condition, the irony being that social media was supposed to be liberating and bring people together, which it manifestly has not.

There has been, in recent years, a vast increase in lived-events-per-unit-of-time, so-called time compression. We are living more and faster - but these lived moments are not being integrated into our memories - our experiential selves. No wonder then that we often feel detached and empty - sensations that we try to fill with more and more "lived events", an impulse that the electronically frenzied world of YouTube and other social media platforms are more than happy to satisfy.

The only people who really do well as YouTubers are the extreme extroverts and the con artists (often the same people). The United States is not really the nation it once was, there is no sense of definite place anymore; it's more of an "arena" where the laws are set up to maximize the pleasure-seeking and fortune-seeking capacities of the adult population.

History will likely trace America's peak as having occurred in the first few decades after the Second World War, a time of egalitarianism when life offered abundant opportunities. Back then, non-college grads and college-grads often had similar salaries and there was no need for Tiger Mothering, choosing a selective university, credentialing, or finding the right career path. It was an era of the common man in which if you worked hard, you could make it into the middle-class. If you were reasonably smart, maybe upper-class. There wasn't much income disparity or status striving back then, so being middle-class was a good deal.

****

We can say that YouTube is a medium that allows individuals to explore themselves and enjoy the freedoms and liberties of a democratic society. And that's fair.

But liberty and freedom at some point becomes toxic. On the bottom rungs of society its effects are more negative. If not checked somehow it leads to nihilism and a dog-eats-dog world and everybody-for-himself world. Poor people in America are more miserable than in other places even though they are so much richer materially. And what can counterbalance it? Respect for hierarchy, customs, traditions, structure. These can provide a sense of community one doesn't see in the sphere of pop culture, YouTube, or political correctness.

We could use more modesty as well, as opposed to the arrogance of believing that our opinion matters and thus must be voiced at every opportunity.

The First Amendment to the Constitution of the United States (freedom of speech) is just a right but not an obligation. Harmony in society would be better achieved when we speak less (i.e., less social media) but listen more.

Welcome to post-Christian America. How do you like it so far?

6.7 School Admission by Merit

Meritocracy and capitalism go hand in hand, you can't have one without the other. In their purest forms each allows the most capable and hard working to succeed. The society which results truly allows each individual to live up to his/her full potential.

Capitalism is bad when it is coupled with lawlessness (like China or Russia) or becomes crony capitalism (much of the west).

Meritocracy is bad when it is coupled with nepotism (e.g., legacy admissions as practiced at Ivy League schools), then it is no longer a true meritocracy.

Unfortunately, thanks to human nature both capitalism and meritocracy will always be in danger of being corrupted. That's why strong laws must be in place and a clean government must be around to enforce these laws.

Harvard practices bad meritocracy that is corrupted by nepotism and diversity admits, but New York City's schools practice true meritocracy in admission to the most sought-after schools. It doesn't get any fairer than going strictly by standardized test results.

If you don't like that too many Asians are getting in, start deporting them. Many of those students who are in NYC are most certainly illegals or children of illegals. Do the same with the Hispanic kids. Then there will be plenty of room left for black and Jewish kids.

Change the immigration law. Do not change the method of admission.

6.8 Privileges for the Already-Privileged

One of the great things about America is that it always finds ways to make the rich even richer and extend more privileges to the already-privileged. And its not just favorable tax treatment and celebrity endorsement deals.

So, when the Duke and Duchess of Sussex were at loose ends wondering where to settle permanently in North America, their dilemma tugged at the heart strings of celebrities. Madonna, beside herself with worry, quickly offered them the use of her Manhattan condo after being filled with compassion at the thought of the Royals adrift in New York City without high-end accommodation, chauffeurs, nannies, and personal stylists.

And when the national media need TV journalists and on-air "personalities" who do they hire? Struggling, young, talented-but-impoverished recent grads? Oh, hell no. They hire people like Democrat party apologist Chris Wallace (son of Mike Wallace) or Anderson Cooper, Gloria Vanderbilt's kid. When NBC's Today show needed a co-host for Hoda Kotb they conducted a nation-wide talent hunt, received thousands of resumes and, with the help of an external consultant, whittled the number down to a manageable short list. No, wait a minute - - - they didn't. Actually, they just gave the job to George W. Bush's daughter Jenna Bush Hagar. I guess Chelsea Clinton was unavailable.

And who was hired to co-host Live! With Kelly and Michael? A football player of course, Hall-of-Famer Michael Strachan and he's Black so a "two-fer". Who else could possibly be qualified? Have to get the right guy: imagine the consequences of having an unqualified TV personality on set. Dodged a bullet there.

When new talk shows are required, who gets to host? Fresh-faces, with impressive academic credentials and conservative views? Of course not! No, those "jobs" go to people like singer Kelly Clarkson and actress Drew Barrymore where their shows provide them a venue to invite their celebrity friends and talk about themselves, their favourite topic.

You can never have too many talk shows.

Then there's the talent-search shows like *American Idol* or *America's got Talent*. These shows perform the important task of identifying the next generation of lounge singers for the Holiday Inn in Fort Wayne Indiana. There are a great many professional musicians, voice coaches, and choreographers etc. who would be terrific judges and panelists on these shows but, naturally, the nod has to go to already well-known, already-wealthy, but over-the-hill minor celebs like Howie Mandel and Paula Abdul.

6.9 Positive Role Models for Kids

Quick, who is a well-known, current-generation public figure who could be considered a positive role model for today's children? You know, someone you would like your children to emulate?

Can't think of anyone, well don't feel bad, neither can I. There certainly isn't anyone who leaps to mind. I would have to think about it for a while. Perhaps a long while.

There used to be role models, well-known public figures that mom and dad pointed to. America had lots of them: Chuck Yeager, John Glenn, Neil Armstrong, Arnold Palmer, Jack Nicklaus, Ernie

Banks, Linus Pauling, Martin Luther King, Ted Williams, Billy Graham, Jim Thorpe, Eric Heiden and so on. You could add in firefighters, police officers, and members of the military.

Canadians had them too: Montreal Canadians Captain Jean Beliveau, hockey players Gordie Howe, Bobby Hull, Bobby Orr, Nobel laureate and one-time prime minister Lester Pearson, Neurosurgeon Wilder Penfield, pianist Glenn Gould, singer Gordon Lightfoot, writer and Nobel laureate Alice Munro and others.

Perhaps it just a sign of the times: we live in a more cynical, aloof, and self-absorbed age. We give little thought to the perpetuation of lineage, culture, or nation; we take our heritage for granted. We are ahistorical and consider the concept of role-models as antiquated notions rooted in the dusty past.

People are more concerned and anxious about their financial situation and social status these days as well. Other people are viewed as competitors or seen in a mercenary sort of way. And genuine friendships seem to be on the decline.

Nevertheless, I believe we need role models, people who could have a calming effect on the rancor and divisiveness that permeates North American culture today.

Role models for kids might be a relic of the dusty past but sometimes the Dark Ages don't seem all that dark.

Chapter 7

CANADIAN IMMIGRATION POLICY

7.1 The Century Initiative and 100 Million Canadians by the Year 2100

Introduction

Usually when a country is a global leader in some area the achievement is noted and proclaimed with pride by its citizens. Alas, not necessarily in the case of Canada and immigration. Even though no country brings in as many immigrants, on a per capita basis and from as many different places, apparently Canada is not doing enough. In fact, it is not doing nearly enough according to the Advisory Council on Economic Growth and its so-called "Century Initiative."

The Advisory Council, comprising fourteen mostly libertarian, globalist, open-border enthusiasts, released a report in the Fall of 2016 calling for Canada to set a population target of 100 million by the year 2100, requiring an immigration intake of 450,000 annually or almost twice the current number. The aim is expedited economic growth and to make Canada more "relevant" internationally.

Quality of Life

Global economic and quality-of-life indicators clearly demonstrate that there is no necessary correlation between population size and a nation's economic strength or other aspect of its desirability. Of the twenty countries with the highest per-capita GDP, only the United States has more than 100 million people. And of the ten highest-ranked countries for quality of life according to research conducted by the Organization for Economic Cooperation and Development (OECD), only two countries, the United States and the United Kingdom, even rank in the top 50 in the world for population size. See Table 1.

Table 1: Ten Highest-Ranked Countries for Quality of Life

Country	Quality of Life Ranking	Population Ranking
Australia	1	51
Sweden	2	89
Canada	3	38
Norway	4	117
Switzerland	5	99
United States	6	3
Denmark	7	112
Netherlands	8	65
Iceland	9	173
United Kingdom	10	22

Source: OECD

Population growth does not create wealth or higher per-capita incomes. These require innovation, entrepreneurship, venture capital, supportive government policies, and productivity improvements gained by coupling modern plant and equipment with a skilled and motivated work force. None of this, per se, has anything to do with population size or population growth.

Consider Sweden: with fewer than 10 million people it has produced 30 Nobel Laureates, far and away the best per-capita performance of any country. It ranks as the seventh-richest country in the world in terms of GDP per capita, and combined public-and-private sector spending on research and development is 3.5 percent of GDP, the second highest in the world. Sweden also is the birthplace of many world-class companies including Volvo, Ericsson, IKEA, and Electrolux. As of 2014, Swedish inventors held 47,112 patents: only ten other countries hold more.

Births and Fertility

The total fertility rate in Canada has been below replacement level for over 40 years and immigration has had a negligible effect on this. Table 2 shows, for example, that while Canada's population increased by over 4.2 million between 2001-2016 (two-thirds of which is attributable to immigration) the fertility rate remained static.

Table 2: Canada's Total Fertility Rate and Population 2001-2016

Year	Fertility Rate	Population
2001	1.60	31,020,596
2006	1.61	31,612,897
2011	1.61	34,342,780
2016	1.61	35,286,425

Source: Statistics Canada: CANSIM, table 102-4505

Younger, recently arrived immigrants make up only a small proportion of the population. To offset the natural age progression of Canada's population, impossibly large numbers of Immigrants would be required. Births in Canada number about 390,000 annually, thus another 95,000 would be necessary to move the fertility rate from the current 1.61 to the replacement level of 2.0 Using immigration to achieve this would require drastic measures such as establishing a special category comprising young couples under the age of 35 with at least two pre-school age children. This would inject the requisite number of children into the 0-4 and 5-9 age cohorts if done every year but would require almost 200,000 additional immigrant spots. And these immigrants would deserve similar consideration to that of Canadian citizens and permanent residents who annually sponsor 15-20,000 parents and grandparents under the Family Class category. All told, Canada's annual intake would rise to over 500,000, which is more than the level advocated by the Century Initiative.

It is not known whether attracting enough young couples under the age of 35 would even be possible. Canada must compete with other nations for quality immigrants and such candidates would want to qualify for reasons other than merely to address Canada's infant shortfall i.e., they would need to otherwise demonstrate a propensity for success.

The alternative to using immigrants to provide more young children would be to obtain a higher yield from the existing female demographic. Since there are about 4.95 million Canadian women of child-bearing age about two percent of them would need to bear a child for the first time (or bear additional children) to achieve the desired 95,000 additional infants. Whether this would be possible with a program of subsidies or tax-incentives is unknown. Women currently forego or limit childbearing for a variety of reasons including the cost and the prospect that children might damage their economic future and career opportunities. With the average cost of a single-family home now more than $500,000 nationally, the situation is not improving.

The Labour Force

The Labour Force Replacement Ratio (LFRR) for Canada has been in decline for more than twenty years and will continue to decline for the foreseeable future. See Table 3.

Table 3: Canada's Labour Force Replacement Ratio 1991-2011

1991	1996	2001	2006	2011
1.43	1.39	1.16	0.96	0.84

Canada can begin to address this in several ways. A key to keeping the labour market adequately supplied will be to find ways to keep the rising tide of senior's participation going. The single most important effort involves the use of technological and efficiency advances and investment in upgraded facilities and equipment to expand the per-worker productive capacity. Canada's labour productivity rate --- the amount of economic output produced per hour worked --- is 25 percent below U.S. levels and below averages for G7 countries so there is much room for improvement.

Concluding Remarks

Canada is not a young country. It existed as a nation for decades before any Canadian living today was born. Neither is Canada an unexplored mystery. We have identified the best natural harbors; the best agricultural lands and where mineral resources are situated. We have built the Trans-Canada highway network and an intercontinental railroad. The best locations for military bases and airfields. have been developed as have the best trans-shipment points (e.g., Thunder Bay). If there were reasons for Cranbrook, British Columbia or North Bay Ontario to be cities of a million-plus people they would be that size already or well on their way.

Does Canada have demographic issues of concern? Absolutely. But what is really needed is a national population policy, one based on objectives that identify how large a population Canada needs and in what areas of the country newcomers are needed and prepared to settle. At a minimum, at least, there needs to be a frank and meaningful dialogue between the federal and provincial governments with a view to adjusting immigration levels to changing conditions in the economy and labour market.

Increasing immigration dramatically using a status-quo approach, as advocated by the Century Initiative, will simply give us a larger version of present-day Canada i.e., more young people and more workers, but more seniors as well. It will do nothing to benefit rank-and-file Canadians and there is every reason to believe that it will lead to a diminished quality of life in our largest cities.

References

[i] Retrieved from: whichcountry.co/top-10-countries-with-highest-quality-of-life.

[i] % of GDP: Research and Development Expenditure statistics – countries compared" NationMaster.com 1 April 2007.

[i] Patents by Country, Sate, and Year – All Patent Types (December 2014) U.S. Patent and Trademark Office. (Retrieved 17 February 2016)

[i] Canada's Aging Population: The Municipal role in Canada's demographic shift" Federation of Canadian Municipalities 2013. p. 10.

[i] Parkinson, David, Janet McFarland, and Barry McKenna. Boom Bust and Economic Headaches. The Globe and Mail 05 January. 2017.

Manufactured by Amazon.ca
Bolton, ON